metalcraft
20 modern projects for the contemporary home

metalcraft

20 modern projects for the contemporary home

Mary Maguire

First edition for the United States, its territories and dependencies, and Canada published in 2006 by Barron's Educational Series, Inc.

First published in Great Britain in 2005 by
Collins & Brown
The Chrysalis Building
Bramley Road
London W10 6SP

An imprint of **Chrysalis** Books Group

All inquiries should be addressed to:
Barron's Educational Series, Inc.
250 Wireless Boulevard
Hauppauge, NY 11788
www.barronseduc.com

ISBN-13: 978-0-7641-3236-0
ISBN-10: 0-7641-3236-9

Library of Congress Catalog Card Number: 2004116541

Designer: Gemma Wilson
Commissioning editor: Marie Clayton
Photographer: Peter Williams

Reproduction by Anorax Imaging Ltd.
Printed by Kyodo Printing Ltd., Singapore

9 8 7 6 5 4 3 2 1

contents

Introduction

Metalwork can be seen as rather cold, hard, and just for men, so in this book I have deliberately set out to make it as user-friendly, feminine, colorful, and textural as possible. Employing familiar and readily available materials such as kitchen foil and food and beverage cans makes metal more approachable. By using some of the fabulous new knitted wires, I have introduced the techniques, color, and texture more associated with feminine crafts.

The metals I have used in the projects have been limited to those that can be cut with ordinary household scissors or with metal shears, thus avoiding some of the harder and more hazardous metalwork techniques. This also makes it possible to tackle all of the projects on a kitchen table—although some protective measures will need to be taken when working with sharp edges, so wear gloves and cover your work surface.

The projects have been designed for a range of skills, from beginner to experienced crafter. If you are a total beginner I suggest starting with partial projects to build up your ability. Try making a few of the butterflies from the wall sconce to use in flower arrangements or as gift tags, or embossing small metal foil squares with a ball point pen to stick onto greeting cards. Many of the projects are much easier than they may look—the wall sconce, mirror, and star for instance—and there are templates provided at the back of the book to help you.

Some of the projects will require a little patience to master the techniques. Molding the round basketlike shapes of the wire-mesh lanterns into beautifully symmetrical forms requires skill and dexterity, offering a challenge to even more experienced craft makers. Like all crafts, practice makes perfect.

The projects are here to inspire you; if they are not quite how you would like them, adapt them to suit your own needs and taste and the materials and tools that you have available. Once you have mastered the techniques in this book, enjoy! You will be able to create new ideas and designs of your own.

Equipment you will need

Before you go and buy all the equipment featured here, check which projects you are going to make. Some of the tools shown—the riveter, for instance—are only used for one project. Assess how much you are going to make and whether you can improvise with what you have already. Scissors, hammer, pliers, and wire cutters are the most essential tools, which you will probably have in your toolbox.

1 Small block of wood: for bracing against metal sheet when folding it.

2 Masking tape: for marking/masking and positioning.

3 Metal shears: will cut through cookie tins and food cans easily.

4 File: when you have used a hammer and nail to make a hole, use the file to smooth away metal burrs.

5 Chisel: a narrow one to pierce holes in metal for the Luminous Lantern (pages 64–70) and Flowery Mirror (pages 74–77). You only need an inexpensive one.

6 Hammer and nails: this is the simplest and easiest way of making holes in metal.

7 Wire cutters: for many of the projects the cutting edge of a pair of pliers is sufficient, but thicker wires and rods need cutters.

8 Pliers: a good pair of pliers is one of the most useful tools to have for the projects in this book.

9 Jewelry pliers: extremely useful little pliers for making small loops and spirals in wire.

10 Paper hole punch: this useful tool will pierce holes in a double sheet of copper foil. It is used for the Wall Light (pages 102–105).

11 Needle-nose pliers: these can get into some areas easier than pliers and are stronger than jewelry pliers if you need to make loops in thicker wire.

12 Paper crinkler: this natty little tool will also put a crinkle in craft foils, copper, and pewter.

13 Screwdriver: available in a range of sizes and with different heads. Choose one to match the type of screws you plan to use.

14 Eyelets: now available in many great colors and funky shapes. Check out good craft shops.

15 Metal thumb tacks: for holding cans in place on the Recycled Utility Rack (pages 50–53).

16 Paper studs and fasteners: we show two types of fasteners, a simple brass one and a larger silver one that has a washer with it. A combination of these were used to make the decoration on the Wall Light (pages 102–105).

17 Glue: use a two-part epoxy glue.

18 Grommet setter: this has a male and female part and is used for setting eyelets or grommets.

19 Teaspoon: this can be used for both smoothing and sculpting areas of thin pewter sheet.

20 Tailor's wheel: there are two types available—blunt and sharp. We have used a sharp one to make rows of pinpricks on the Stunning Star (pages 70–73) and the Wall Light (pages 102–105). You can buy them from a sewing supplies store.

21 Embossing tools: useful if you are going to do a lot of work with pewter. A ballpoint pen is sufficient for most of the projects in this book.

22 Ruler: this can be plastic, metal, or wood, but make sure the dimension markings are clear.

23 Wire twister: this little gadget is designed to twist wire. It can be used for fine wires, but a hand drill is much better. If you don't have one, look at flea markets or second-hand shops.

24 Pop riveter: a good, strong way of fixing two pieces of metal together.

25 Protective gloves: wear when cutting cookie tins and food cans. Jagged edges can be dangerous.

26 Block of wood or an old cutting board: for hammering into to protect your work surface.

27 Craft knife: a strong retractable blade knife is always useful in your tool box. It is used here to cut long strips of aluminum foil.

28 Scissors: ordinary household scissors are sufficient to cut cans, foils, and 0.006 in (0.15 mm) pewter sheet. For a couple of projects pinking shears have been used to give a zig-zag edge.

29 Can opener: an ordinary can opener as used in the kitchen is fine.

Materials you will need

Good craft shops will be able to supply colored aluminum foil and some wires. For a wide range of wires, copper, pewter, brass, and foils see the list of suppliers in the back of this book. Galvanized wire can be bought in various gauges from hardware, gardening, or do-it-yourself (DIY) shops.

1 Pewter foil: this is a beautiful material to work with. It is made of 95% tin, 4% antimony, and 1% copper. The sheets used for the projects in this book are 0.006 in (0.152 mm) thick. These sheets are so soft that they can be embossed, sculpted, folded, pleated, and hammered. It is costly, so it's advisable to buy a 12 in (30 cm) square to experiment with before buying a roll.

2 Rolls of craft wire: these come in amazing zingy colors and a range of gauges. It is worth buying large rolls if you are going to do a lot of wire work.

3 Permanent felt-tipped pens: as long as your metal is grease-free and clean, these will color adequately for the projects in this book. But if you need a hardwearing finish for constant handling, you can buy metal paints instead.

4 Galvanized garden wire: this is available in a range of gauges from hardware and garden stores.

5 Knitted tubular wire: available in two gauges and a wide range of colors from the suppliers listed at the back of the book. It can be stretched vertically and horizontally and also shaped.

6 Assorted beads: wooden beads are used for the handle in the Bead Holder (pages 88–93), and glass beads for the Jewelry Tree (pages 58–63).

7 Elastic: round elastic used for the projects in this book can be purchased in large stationery stores, gift stores, or fabric stores.

8 Metal rods: available from model makers' shops in a range of different gauges and metals.

9 Spring wire (bouillon thread, tanka, or spaghetti wire): These are hollow springlike threads of colored metal, which is used for the Wire-Mesh Flowers (pages 98–101). It comes in smooth and faceted, and is available in mixed packs of different gauges and colors, or packs of all the same.

10 Aluminum wire: thick ⅛ in (3.25 mm) aluminum wire, very soft, easy to bend, and to color. It is available from the suppliers listed at the back of the book (page 127).

11 Aluminum craft foil: this is thicker than kitchen foil, which gives a wider range of possibilities for construction. It is color coated on one side only. It is easy to emboss and interesting to put through a ribbling machine.

12 Coils of craft wire: this is the same wire as on the reels, but it is also available in large coils and in small or mixed bags of random assorted colors.

13 Copper sheeting: this is thicker than aluminum craft foil. It is still easily cut with household scissors and holes can be made using a paper punch. It is available in rolls.

14 Brass: this is harder and springier than copper, so although you can emboss into it, it is not as yielding as copper or pewter.

Basic techniques
Cutting small shapes in metal

This can be done very easily when working with foils and the metal from beverage cans, but it gets a bit harder when it comes to thicker cans, where you must use metal shears.

1 Don't go straight for the detail. Cut out the general shape first (as shown on the background flower). Then work around the flower, cutting the curves in one direction only at first, as shown.

2 Next work around the flower in the opposite direction, carefully removing the surplus material as shown. Finally, neaten up the rough edges where the cutting strokes meet.

*The flowers are used for this lovely
Flowery Mirror on page 74.*

Making holes

There are various ways to make holes in metal; the three methods in this book are very simple.

Paper punch

Surprisingly, a simple paper hole punch can make holes in thin metal foils or the aluminum from cans. It will even punch through two layers of copper foil.

Hammer and nail

The simplest way to make a hole in tin is to use a hammer and nail. Nails come in different sizes, from tiny panel pins to big masonry nails. They leave a ragged edge, however, which must be filed smooth. Protect your surface when making a hole this way.

Tracing wheel

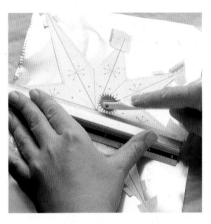

This natty tool allows you to make a line of evenly-spaced pinprick holes. You can work with a ruler for straight lines or freehand for curved. Tracing wheels can be purchased from a good sewing store or fabric shop.

Chisels

Chisels come with different-sized sharp ends and can be used for cutting slots. Hold the chisel firmly in position and hit the handle hard with a hammer.

Filing

A file will smooth off any rough edges made when hammering a hole with a nail or chisel. Just file away the jagged pieces.

The Stunning Star light on page 70 features holes made in several different ways.

Working with foils

Foil is sheet metal that has been very thinly rolled out. The most accessible and familiar version is aluminum kitchen foil, which is silver-colored with one side matte, the other shiny. Aluminum embossing craft foil is much stronger; images can be drawn or pressed into it without risk of it tearing easily. It is available in different sumptuous colors on one side and silver on the other. Thicker still are copper, brass, and pewter foils, which are available in limited thicknesses from craft suppliers. If you want to develop your work and use a wider range you will need a specialist metal supplier.

Regular foil

Aluminum kitchen foil is probably the most readily-accessible metalcraft material. It is surprisingly versatile and can be used to produce interesting crafts.

Crinkling

If you want a sheet of crinkled foil, wad a sheet of foil up into a ball—but don't make it too tight, because it will be impossible to unroll.

Hammering

Scrunched up foil can be hammered until it is really compacted, making it a very hard material.

Smoothing

The surface of your sculpted foil can be smoothed by rubbing it over glass or a mirror many times.

These pretty Foil Night Light Holders are on page 24.

Craft foil

Craft embossing foil is thicker than kitchen foil and doesn't tear as easily, so it is more robust. It's also available in fabulous colors.

Crinkling

These little crinkling machines are great fun and easy to use with paper or foil. Place the smooth foil into the machine, wind the handle, and out comes corrugated foil—you can do several layers together.

Pleating

This is a tedious job. You need to get your nails between each crinkle and push them together, then work outwards, gathering in a pair of pleats at a time.

Compacting

If you want to crush foil or compact it into a neat circle, use pliers for the central arms and top of the skirt on the Dancing Dolls. Needle-nose pliers give you a greater width range than ordinary pliers. Use the round recess in pliers (but not the cutting edge) to compress the skirt top.

The brightly colored Dancing Dolls on page 34 are made from craft foils.

Embossing

It is important to work on a yielding surface—the more yielding the surface, the deeper you will be able to emboss. A mouse pad, padded envelope, or folded towel are all good surfaces to use. All the foils used in this book can be cut with household scissors. There are special tools available for embossing, with different heads to give varying qualities of line. If you want to develop the art it is worth investing in these; otherwise a ballpoint pen is perfectly sufficient for any of the projects in this book. You can work freehand or with a template. With pewter, copper, and brass—which are a lot more expensive than craft foil—it is preferable to use a template until you are really experienced.

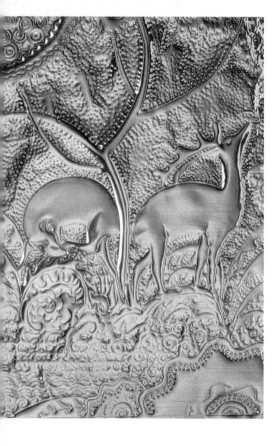

Straight Lines

Use a ruler or straightedge to draw any straight lines. Keep your pressure even and try to make the line continuous rather than stopping and starting, which leads to irregularity in the texture.

Curves

It's a good idea to copy the template several times and practice going over it. Long sweeping curves are the hardest to do and mistakes will be most noticeable on them. Keep your wrist loose and practice making sweeping curves generally with paper and ballpoint pen until your line becomes confident.

Rounding Out

Once your pattern is embossed you can reverse it and further heighten the relief from the back. Broad areas can be smoothed over and pushed with your finger.

A detail of the attractive Embossed Tray on page 54.

Filling

Pewter is so malleable that the relief can easily be flattened; to support the design the back needs to be filled with a solid medium. Here we have used slightly watered-down plaster filler which has been spread on the underside of the design. Its surface has then been skimmed with a flexible ruler to remove the excess, and to only leave filler in the recesses.

Turning corners

Making metal foil wrap around corners neatly requires both patience and skill. Practice on some scraps first.

1 To turn a curved corner, use jewelry pliers. Make sure you have enough excess border to wrap around the base. Twist a kink in either side of the corner using the jewelry pliers, as shown.

2 Continue to work around the corner, closing up all the excess metal between these two kinks by making even corrugations which should stand up at 45°.

3 Repeat Steps 1 and 2 on each of the other three corners as shown above.

4 Use your jewelry pliers to grip the central corrugation and pull it down over the corner. Repeat with each groove on either side.

5 Use a teaspoon to iron out and flatten the turned metal. Rub along the folds with the convex side of the spoon. Fit the side of the corner into the concave part of the spoon and rub along and around it.

These unusual Pewter Coasters are featured on page 30.

Cutting metals

Many food and beverage cans can be cut with ordinary household scissors. For thicker metals, such as cookie tins and more solid food cans, you will need either tin snips or metal shears.

A combination of beverage and food cans are the basis for the Recycled Utility Rack on page 50.

Cutting open cookie tins

As you use bigger tins the potential for hurting yourself is greater because the size makes them more unwieldy, so make sure you use protective gloves.

1 Cut vertically down along the side rim, then horizontally along the bottom edge. It is difficult to get a neat cutting line at this stage, but it can be neatly trimmed later. Keep rolling back the cut-away metal, as shown, to get your cutters as far in as possible.

2 Draw the size of the hole you want first, then make a "V" shaped slot in the center with a hammer and chisel. Push this "v" out, or pull out with pliers. Insert the jaws of your metal shears into the hole and, cutting in a gradual spiral, work your way around until you have reached the marked line of the shape you want to cut out.

Cutting open beverage cans

1 As the rim is the hardest part, pierce just below it with a knife or the single blade of a pair of scissors.

2 Insert the scissors and cut around the can along the edge of the rim, to remove the top.

Cutting open food cans

1 Wearing protective gloves, remove the lid on the inside using a top-opening can opener—not a side-opening type. Using metal shears, cut over the rim and straight down the side, then cut along the side of the rim. Continue all the way around if you want a flat piece of metal. If you want a 3-D half can for the utility rack, cut a quarter way along one side of the vertical cut and a quarter way the other side. Then, bracing the metal against a wooden block, force this metal back as shown.

2 Once you have folded back both side flaps you will need to remove half of the bottom of the can in line with the flaps and half of the top rim.

Wire

For the projects in this book we have used three types of wire, but there are many more available from specialists. The most accessible wire is galvanized garden wire, which comes in a good range of thicknesses and can be bought from hardware/DIY or gardening shops. It can be bent with pliers and cut with wirecutters. We have used it for making hooks, catches, hinges, and handles in many of the projects.

Aluminum wire is softer and can be easily bent with your hands. It is light in weight and can be colored with permanent felt-tipped pens. It is used for the Butterfly Wall Sconce on page 82.

Craft wire is a malleable copper wire coated in fabulous colored finishes and is available in a wide range of gauges. The knitted mesh is made from it and we have used it for the Dancing Dolls on page 34, the Jewelry Tree on page 58, and the Butterfly Wall Sconce on page 82.

Bending wire

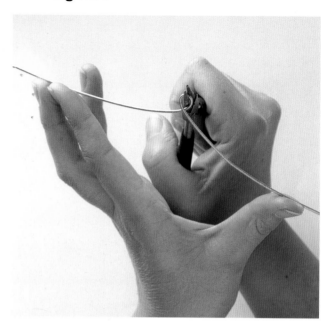

To make a loop, bend, or a small curve in wire, you can use jewelry pliers. If you want the loop to be central, as shown here, position the pliers in the middle of the wire, wrap each end over the nose, and press the ends away.

Larger bends

If you want an evenly curved bend, use a former. This can be anything from a pencil to a broomhandle to a tin can (shown here). Force your wire around it with even pressure.

Making spirals

Start by making a loop in one end of your wire; use jewelry pliers for a small loop and needle-nose pliers for larger loops. Draw the wire around into a spiral.

Twisting wires

Two or more wires can be twisted, either for extra strength or for decorative reasons. This can be particularly effective when you use different colored wires. It can be done most effectively with a hand drill.

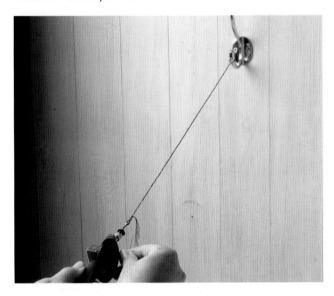

1 Bind or loop the wires around the end of a stable wall hook. Make sure the ends you are twisting are equal length, then insert them securely into the jaws of your drill, or wrap them around a hook held in your drill. Keep the wires taut while twisting.

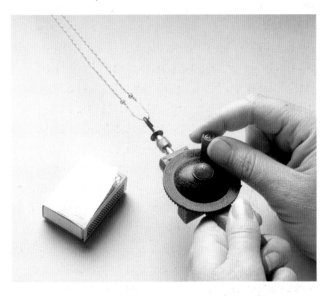

2 If you want to twist together two strands of already-twisted wire, the easiest way is to bend the twisted wires in half. Put the loop on the hook, then insert the ends into the jaws of your drill, as in Step 1. Again, keep the wires taut while twisting.

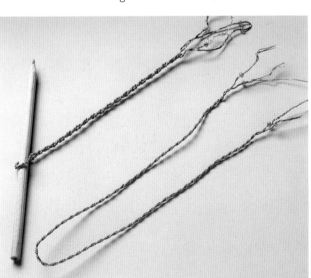

3 On short lengths it is just as easy to use a pencil. Group all twisted wires together and thread onto a pencil. Clutch the other end securely with pliers, then slowly twist the pencil.

This brightly colored Jewelry
Tree is on page 58.

Coloring metals

There are special paints and inks devised for metal, but in this book we have used enamel paint for two projects, and for all the rest we've used permanent felt-tipped pens—which are bright, effective, and easy to use. They work well on items that don't need to be handled too much. It is important that the metal surface is clean and grease-free before using.

Enamel paint

Cover your work surface and surrounding areas and follow the manufacturer's instructions on the can.

Felt-tipped pens

The delicate Butterfly Wall Sconce on page 82 is colored with brightly luminous, permanent felt-tip pens.

Make sure the metal is clean and totally grease-free. Do not touch the areas of metal as you color them.

Riveting metals

Riveting is a very effective way of joining two metal surfaces together. First, you will need to make a hole in both surfaces, which can be done by drilling or with a hammer and nail. If you follow the latter course, make sure you file smooth the edges of the hole afterwards.

1 Hold the surface to be riveted securely. Insert the rivet into the nozzle, then into the matching holes, and squeeze the riveter firmly. This is the hardest part because it will require a lot of strength in your hands.

Rivets are used both to decorate and fix the Wall Light on page 102.

2 When you are riveting a thicker surface or through more layers, choose extra-long rivets.

Foil night light
holders

Foil is a surprisingly strong and
versatile material and can be used
for simple or serious sculpting.
By twisting, shaping, compressing, and
hammering it becomes a solid metal
shape that is texturally interesting
and light in color and weight.
These hearts have been formed
with a recess just large enough to
fit a night light into, for use as a
romantic table decoration.

YOU WILL NEED:

- 1 roll kitchen foil
- Piece of card
- Piece of silver card
- Double-sided tape
- Masking tape
- Night light

EQUIPMENT:

- Scissors
- Hammer
- Smooth surface

1 Using the template on page 124, cut out a card heart to make the base. Unroll your kitchen foil and fold it over to make a strip 1⅜ in (3.5 cm) wide. Fold this over five times, smoothing it each time with your fingers. Cut this strip away from the roll.

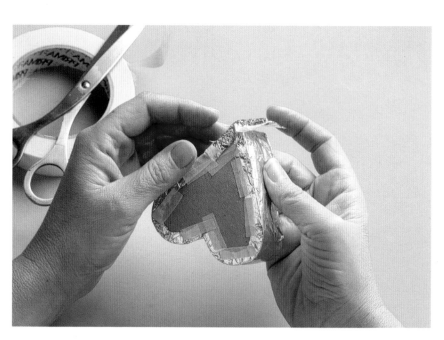

2 Fold a margin ¼ in (6 mm) along one long edge of this strip of foil. Wrap the strip around the heart shape and tape the margin to the card base.

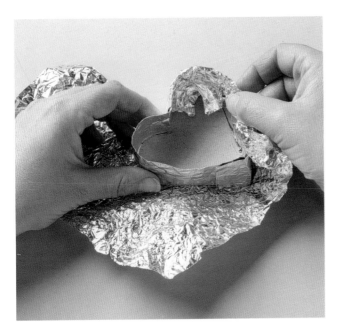

3 Referring to the Basic Techniques on page 14, tear some larger pieces of foil. Scrunch them up and then smooth out. Place the heart on these and wrap the foil around, pinching in around the wall of the heart to reinforce it. Repeat this with several more layers.

4 Fold over several layers of foil to form strips the same depth as the night light. Wrap loosely around the night light and tape into a ring (you must be able to remove the night light easily). Fill the bottom of the heart with pieces of foil and place the night light and surround inside so that the top is level with the top of the heart.

5 Rip small pieces of foil and wad up into small balls. Pack the inside of the heart with these without distorting its shape.

6 Use a hammer to really compact the foil. As it squashes down, push more pieces in.

7 Scrunch up some large sheets of foil and smooth out again, as in Step 3.

8 Remove the night light, then wrap the sheets of foil loosely over the top of your heart, allowing enough slack to line the recess. Press into the sides with your fingertips. Wrap the remainder around the sides and take to the back.

9 Gather up the excess foil and squash it evenly around the back. Hammer it down to flatten.

10 Use a piece of glass, mirror, or a similar material, to rub all over the surface of the heart to make it smooth. Press firmly while doing this.

11 Cut out another heart in silver card and stick it to the bottom of the holder using double-sided tape.

Pewter
coasters

These pewter coasters, reminiscent of the art deco style, have been made by embossing patterns onto pewter foil from provided templates. This is an easy process and can be done simply with an old ballpoint pen or embossing tool. The difficult part is achieving smooth flat corners; this requires practice, and because pewter is quite a costly material, it is more economical to practice on a piece of copper sheeting.

You can also make greeting cards with this technique. Draw a motif into your pewter foil and cut it out with straight-edged or pinking shears before attaching it to a card with strong double-sided tape.

YOU WILL NEED:

- 1 set of old coasters
- 0.06 in (0.15 mm) thickness pewter foil
- Plaster
- Velcro
- Template on page 120

EQUIPMENT:

- Scissors
- Ballpoint pen
- Ruler
- Jewelry pliers
- Teaspoon
- Padded envelope (or other yielding surface, such as a mouse pad)

1 Cut out a piece of pewter large enough to cover your coaster (with at least ½ inch [or 1 cm] margin all around). Put the pewter on the padded envelope and place your coaster on top. Draw a line all around the edge. This side will be the inside.

2 Remove the coaster and turn the piece of pewter over; this will be the outside. Tape the template within the embossed border. Using a ruler, mark in all the straight lines.

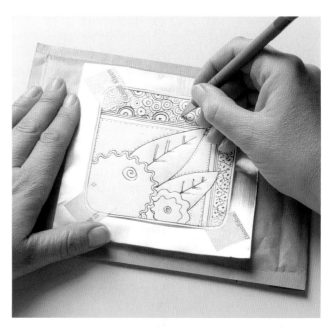

3 Continue to draw in all the major lines, then put in the detail.

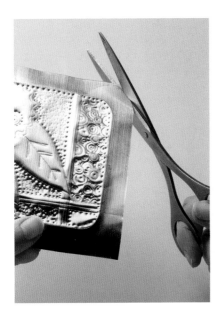

4 Round off the corners using scissors.

5 Place the coaster onto the "inside" of the pewter; make sure you position it accurately. Then turn up the sides as shown. Referring to Basic Techniques (page 17), follow the instructions for corrugating corners.

6 Once the corners have been corrugated, spread plaster thinly over the design and leave it to dry.

7 Fold in the sides and pull the corners over a little at a time. Try to space them evenly using jewelry pliers, as shown. Check all the time that the outside edge is smooth.

8 Using the concave part of the spoon, rub along and around the outside corner's edge. Then use the convex side to press and smooth down the pleated edge on the base (as in the Basic Techniques, page 17).

9 If your coasters have cork bottoms like these, press indentations all around the edge using a ballpoint pen. This will help secure the pewter. Place a coaster on a piece of sticky-backed felt and draw around it. Cut this out, remove the backing, and carefully press it into position.

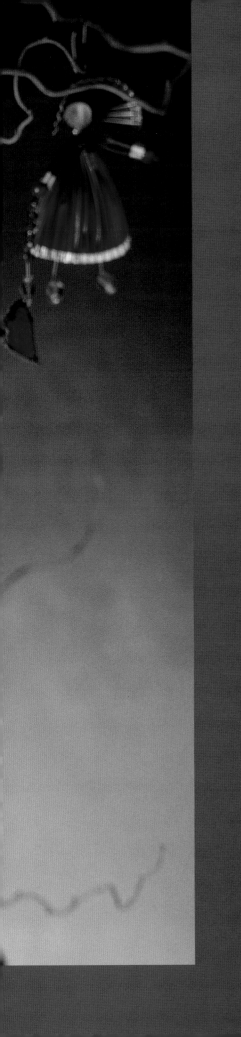

Dancing
dolls

These delightful little dollies can be made as Christmas ornaments, party decorations, or birthday celebrations. Hang them from a Christmas tree branch or mantle shelf so their legs wobble and their beaded bowers sway.

The craft foil has been put through a crinkling machine, which corrugates it. This also makes the foil much more rigid, giving more strength to construct your dolls with.

Twirly strips can be made to complement the dolls by cutting long tapering strips of foil. Put these through the crinkle machine, then form twists by gently spiralling them.

YOU WILL NEED:

- Embossing foils in various colors
- Length of 0.9 mm (20 gauge) wire in red and green
- Beads per doll:
  1 frosted 10 mm foiled lamp bead, 2 6 mm miracle beads, 2 lozenge-shaped Indian beads, 10 round 6 mm beads, 1 seed bead
- For each garland:
  4 gold seed beads,
  6 red gold seed beads,
  8 green seed beads,
  2 crystals,
  4 color lined beads

EQUIPMENT:

- Old ballpoint pen
- Ribbling machine
- Scissors
- Ruler
- Double-sided tape
- Wire cutter
- Pliers (preferably needle-nose, but not essential)
- Jewelry pliers

1 Cut out six pieces of foil to the following dimensions for each doll: for the skirt, 5 × 2 ½ in (12.5 × 6.5 cm); for the arms, 2½ × 1¼ in (6.5 × 3 cm); for the hat, one piece 1½ × 2¼ in (4 × 5.5 cm) and one contrasting color 1¼ × 2¼ in (3 × 5.5 cm); for the heart, two 1 × 1 in (2.5 × 2.5 cm) in contrasting colors. Fold over ⅛ in (3 mm) strip along one long edge of the skirt piece and both short edges of the arm piece and smooth with a finger to form a crisp edge.

2 Sandwich the hat pieces together, back to back, and fold the excess ⅛ in (3 mm) over to make a border. Then run through the ribbling machine, short side first. Run the arm piece through with the widest side first and the skirt piece with the shortest side first.

3 To make the hat, push together the pleats of the unbordered side to form a fan shape. To make the skirt, force together one edge with your nails (as shown), while bowing out in a bell shape beneath with your fingers. All the time move around the top to form it into a circle.

4 Cut a thin strip of double-sided tape and use it to join the two edges of the skirt together. See Basic Techniques for shaping.

5 Roll up the foil "arms" into a cylinder and curve the hat shape as shown.

6 Thread a piece of wire 3½ in (9 cm) long through the arms. Thread a miracle bead onto both ends and make a loop to hold them using jewelry pliers. Flatten the middle (see Basic Techniques page 20).

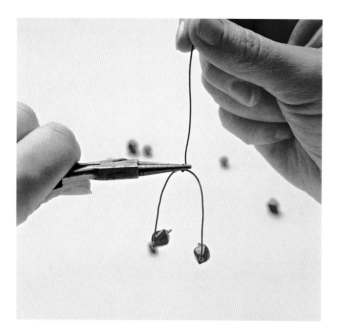

7 Cut a 5¼ in (13 cm) length of wire for the legs and a 2½ in (6.5 cm) length for the body. Thread a lozenge bead onto each end of the leg wire and loop the ends to secure using jewelry pliers. Bend the wire to form the legs. Attach the body wire by making a loop at one end around the leg wire and then pressing closed, as shown.

8 Using a darning needle, pierce a hole through the foil in the middle of the arms. Pierce another one midway along the bottom of the hat.

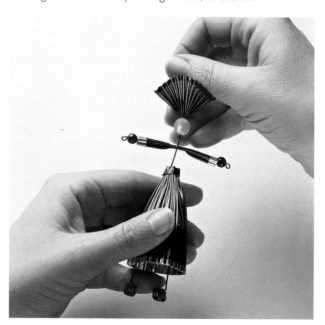

9 Thread the skirt onto the body wire, followed by the arms, bead head, and hat. Form a hanging loop with the excess wire above the hat. Wrap a thin strip of foil backed with double-sided tape around the top of the skirt to make a band.

10 Using the template on page 124, emboss and cut out a heart shape. For each, cut out a larger heart in a contrasting color with pinking shears. Cut 3 lengths of wire: one red 2½ in (6.5 cm) and two green 1½ in (4 cm) long. Place the longer wire between the two hearts and join them all together with double-sided tape.

11 Thread beads onto the wire on both sides of the heart, as shown. Thread the green wires with the remaining beads. Using jewelry pliers, attach the shorter wires to each hand. Use the heart wires to link one doll to another. To hang the dolls, make hooks from 4½ in (11.5 cm) lengths of wire. Attach to the top of each dancer.

Wire-mesh lanterns

These sumptuous colored lanterns are made from tubular knitted wire which has been shaped into basketlike forms, with coiled wire and glass beads decorating the tips. Contrasting colored knitted wire bands have been placed at the necks and rims to add color and texture. Each "basket" has been attached to the lights by threading craft wires through the knitted rim and looping ends over the string of lights. (The lanterns are metal so they will need low voltage lights, or others with a transformer.)

YOU WILL NEED:

(For each individual lantern)

- 7 in (17.5 cm) tubular knitted wire for body
- 2 in (5 cm) tubular knitted wire for rim decoration
- 1 in (2.5 cm) tubular knitted wire for rim decoration
- 2 in (5 cm) tubular knitted wire for neck
- 1 in (2.5 cm) tubular knitted wire for neck
- 1 coil of 0.5 mm (24 gauge) craft wire
- 1 large-holed foil bead
- Length of 0.9 mm (20 gauge) craft wire for attaching to lights

EQUIPMENT:

- Set of fairy lights
- Pliers
- Scissors
- Jewelry pliers

1 Cut a 7 in (17.5 cm) length of knitted tubing. It comes flat, so make it tubular, smoothing the side creases out. Roll down a rim at one end so that the body is the length of your thumb and start pushing the mesh together at the base to taper it in.

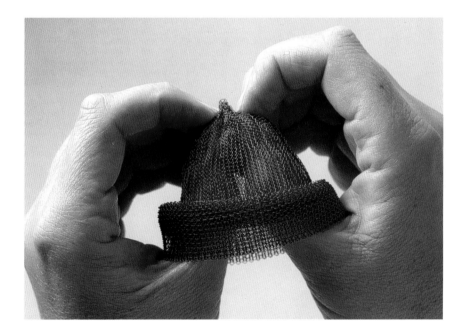

2 Position your thumbs inside the "lantern" and squeeze the tip together with your fingertips.

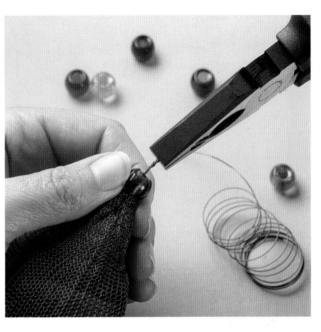

3 Use the indented circle of the cutting jaws (but not the cutting edge) of a pair of pliers to compress this tip into an even cone.

4 Attach a wire through the point of the cone and thread on a bead, using a swivelling action to push it onto the core. Bind the wire around the bead and through the "lantern" at quarterly intervals.

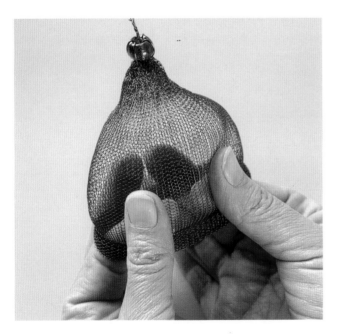

5 Roll down the top without stretching the mesh. Work around the "lantern" making a belly by stretching out slightly until you have an upside-down, onion-shaped dome. The belly should be at its widest at 2½ in (6.5 cm) up from the tip of the cone.

6 Keep rolling back the knitting, then start tapering in from the belly to form a neck, about 3½ in (9 cm) from the tip. Make the neck about ⅓ in (8 mm) deep.

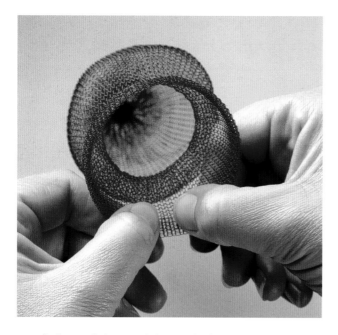

7 Roll out all the remaining mesh above the neck, then fold over the edge three times to make a rim 1/3 in (8 mm) deep.

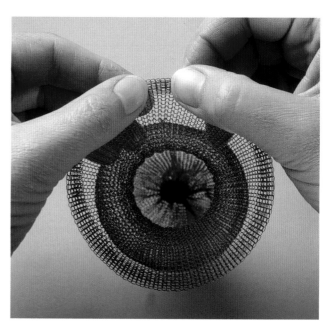

8 Pull this rim out evenly, little by little, working around and around the rim. You want it to lie flat. If it is wavy, you have overstretched it.

9 Attach a piece of contrasting wire and bind the cone tip just above the bead, as shown. Tuck the end inside and snap off excess wire from the attached bead.

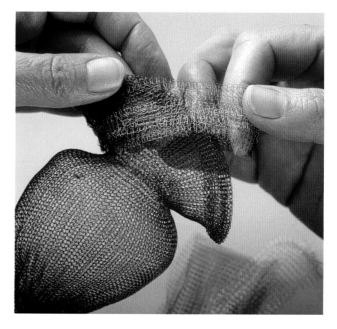

10 To make the neck band, cut two contrasting colors of knitted wire, one 2 in (5 cm) and one 1 in (2.5 cm) wide. Fold the edges of both over a few times. Place the thinner band around the thicker and stretch over the lantern top (fold the top up to help). Position around the neck and push together to make a snug fit.

11 Use another 2 in- (5 cm-) and 1 in- (2.5 cm-) wide piece to make a decorative rim. Fold over the edges of both, then fold each in half. Pull out along the fold so that this becomes the outer edge and then turn over the inner. Insert the rim of the lantern inside the thickest edging first, then the thinner.

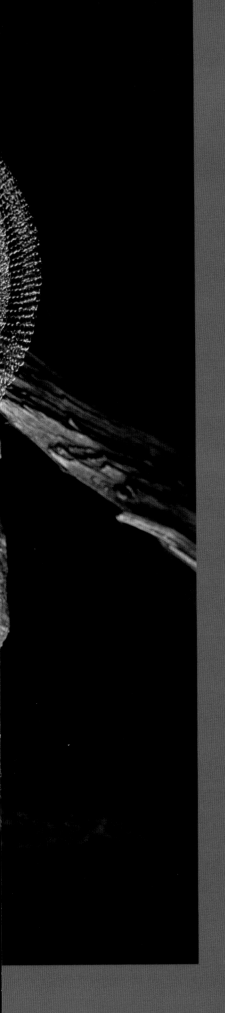

Wire-mesh
jewelry

Make beautiful, eye-catching jewelry that looks really contemporary with knitted tubular wire. These beautiful bracelets can be made easily by following the steps. These instructions show you how to make the purple and green bracelet—they are basically the same design, but different in color and depth.

The dark purple is a variation. It is important to use the thicker gauge wire to make the central core of the bracelet. This will hold the shape best. When putting the bracelets on, don't pull too hard on the edges—this will distort the shapes (although if this happens they can be easily reshaped).

YOU WILL NEED:

(For wide bracelet)

- 8 in (20cm) length emerald green knitted wire 0.2 mm (28 gauge)
- 8 in (20 cm) length turquoise (super green) 0.1 mm (30 gauge)
- 4 in (10 cm) length purple knitted wire 0.1 mm (30 gauge)

(For narrow bracelet)

- 6 in (15 cm) purple knitted wire 0.1 mm (30 gauge)
- 2 in (5 cm) turquoise knitted wire 0.1 mm (30 gauge)
- 2 in (5 cm) aubergine knitted wire 0.1 mm (30 gauge)

1 Cut three lengths of knitted wire for each bracelet. For the wide one, fold over the edges of the green and turquoise three times outwards to make bands 3½ in (9 cm) and 3 in (7.5 cm) wide. Fold both edges of the purple inwards into bands 1 in (2.5 cm) wide. For the narrow one, fold over the edges of the purple three times outwards to make a band 1½ in (4 cm) wide. Roll over turquoise and aubergine to make bands ¼ in (6 mm) and ½ in (15 mm) wide.

2 For the large bracelet, insert the green band inside the turquoise, then position the purple band around the center. For the small bracelet, put the purple band inside the aubergine and the turquoise band on the outside, as shown.

3 Make both the flat tubes round by inserting your fingers and forming them into a tubular shape.

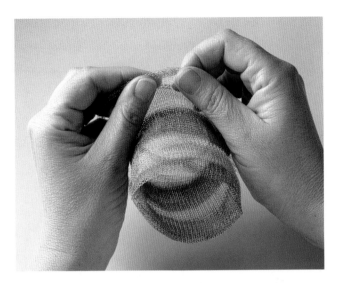

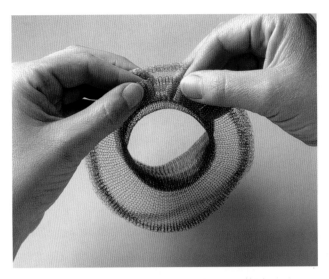

4 On the large bracelet, stretch out the edge of the turquoise band between your fingers and thumbs, and work around the edge little by little to get an even stretch. On the small bracelet, do the same with the purple band.

5 On the large bracelet, stretch out the edge of the green band, stretching to the same amount as before so that both edges fan out evenly. If you overstretch, it will go wavy.

Recycled
utility rack

This delightful 3-D patchwork rack is made from an assortment of interesting cans from around the world.

Every country has its classic cans. Collect them when you go on vacation or look in your local ethnic food stores, grocery stores, and delicatessens. You'll find quite a variety.

The background is mostly made up from the sides of beverage cans, while the 3-D portion (half cut-away) is mostly food cans. Use these to hold your kitchen implements, dish towels (remove top and bottom of the can to hold these), pens, string, and other household objects. The pull ring still found on some can tops can be bent out and used to hang your keys on.

YOU WILL NEED:

- Piece of MDF 24 × 18 in (60 cm × 45 cm) and ½ in (1.5 cm) thick
- 4 glass plates with screws, no longer than the thickness of the MDF
- Approx. 25 assorted beverage cans
- Assorted interesting food cans
- Aluminum embossing foil (optional)
- Thumb tacks
- Copper nails and panel pins

EQUIPMENT:

- Bradawl
- Drill
- Scissors
- Hammer and nails
- Ruler
- Pliers
- Strong double-sided tape

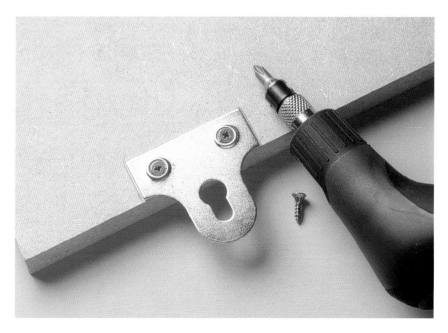

1 Mark suitable positions for your mounting plates on the back of the MDF mounting board. Make a pilot hole through the fixing holes, then screw the plates in place.

2 Cut open a selection of your tin cans as shown in Basic Techniques, page 19, and push them flat. Arrange them in a patchwork around your board, adjusting positions until you get the look you want. Use strong double-sided tape and thumb tacks to hold them in place. If necessary, make pilot holes for the tacks before pushing them in.

3 Arrange the feature cans on top of patchwork. When you are happy with their positions, take one off at a time and cut them down the back as shown in Basic Techniques, page 19. Fold back the sides and cut half of the bottom away.

4 Nail the feature cans into their positions through the side flaps, then cover the flaps with other beverage cans. When using small nails it can help to hold them in position by pushing through a piece of thin card, as shown.

5 Arrange attractive cookie tin lids around the board to complete your collage.

6 Using a metal ruler and a craft knife, cut two strips of aluminum embossing foil 24 x 1½ in (60 x 4 cm) and another two strips 18 x 1½ in (60 x 4 cm). Draw a margin lengthways along each strip, ¼ in (6 mm) in from one edge. Bend the strips along the margin at a right angle.

7 Stick a length of double-sided tape along the edges of the backing board, then position the aluminum strips down each edge with the ¼ in (6 mm) margin making a border around the collage. Rub along the sides of the board to make sure the foil sticks firmly and bend any excess over to the back of the board. Stick parcel tape over the excess foil at the back and hammer copper nails at regular intervals around the front border.

Embossed
tray

Here an embossed art deco-style design has been made to line the bottom of an MDF blank tray. The template for the design is on page 121; this can be enlarged or reduced to fit bigger or smaller projects. You may even want to revamp an old tray.

This is a complex design and needs time and patience to complete. The important lines need to be made with a sweeping confidence—if you fumble with the drawing it will show—so practice first with smaller-scale projects, because pewter is expensive. The design needs to be back-filled once it is finished to protect the 3-D design from squashing flat.

YOU WILL NEED:

- MDF blank tray (or old tray)
- Thin sheet of pewter (size of the bottom of your tray)
- Plaster
- Paint (if emulsion, you will need decorator's matte varnish also)

EQUIPMENT:

- Ballpoint pen
- Yielding surface (such as a padded envelope)
- Ruler
- Embossing tools (optional)
- Double-sided tape

1 Photocopy the template on page 121 to the size of the bottom of your tray. Cut a piece of pewter sheet to the same size and tape the template securely onto the sheet so that it won't move around. Place the sheet with its template onto a yielding surface.

2 Using a ruler and ballpoint pen, start by embossing all the straight lines by drawing over them, pressing firmly into the pewter as you work. Make sure you hold the ruler carefully in position, and that you make clean, decisive lines.

3 Draw in all the main elements of the design—it helps with a detailed design to use a different color from the lines of the template so you will know which lines you have already been over. You need to draw firmly and with confidence.

4 Once all the lines of the design have been traced over, you can put in the texture. It would be exasperating to mark dot for dot, so just dot across the areas generally noting that the dots may be smaller and more intense in some places.

5 Once you have completely embossed your design, remove the template and turn the pewter over. Smooth over the broad flat areas (like the deer) with your finger, to help mold the shape into relief.

6 You can use special embossing tools to further delineate or push some areas into relief—like the ear of the deer, for instance.

7 Mix up some plaster filler with water to a consistency that can be spread easily. Spoon some of this along one side of the design and use a flexible ruler to level and draw the mixture across the pewter sheet, skimming over the surface so that all the recesses are properly filled. Leave to dry.

8 Paint all the sides and underneath your wooden tray in the required color. If you are using a matte emulsion, use a decorator's varnish over the top of it once it is dry to seal the surface. If you use a special paint for wood this is not necessary, as this type of paint will give a harder wearing, wipe-clean surface.

9 Using strong double-sided tape, tape around the edges of the bottom of the tray. Affix your pewter design—you must be very careful to position it accurately first time because repositioning may cause bends and dents in the pewter. Press around the edge with an embossing tool.

Jewelry
tree

Make this cool tree as an ornament or as something to hang your earrings from. Craft wire comes in fab and funky colors. Choose three different colors, as shown here, or three of the same and find beads that will complement your wires. More beads could be used at the end of each wire, to represent flowery blossoms on the tree.

The base of the tree is weighted with a garden stone. Find a heavy (medium potato-sized) one and clean it thoroughly before use.

YOU WILL NEED:

- 3 × 15 ft (1 × 4 m) coils of 0.5 mm (24 gauge) wire in super violet, super green, pink
- Galvanized wire (or other thicker wire) 1.5 mm (14 gauge)
- Beads—20 gms blue/pink color lined Rocailles 6/0
- 100 gms of blue/pink color-lined 2-cuts
- Kitchen foil
- Stone for base
- PVA adhesive

EQUIPMENT:

- Wire cutters
- Hand drill or wire winder
- Pencil
- Jewelry pliers
- Bowl and spoon

1 Cut five 45 in (113 cm) lengths of wire in each color so that you have 15 lengths in total. Group in five bunches, with each having three different colored wires. Thread 4 Rocaille beads onto each bunch.

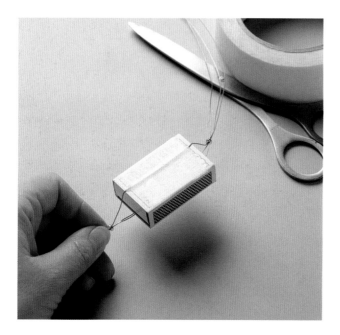

2 Midway along the length of one of the bunches fix a matchbox or similar shape with masking tape, with the wires running on either side as shown above. Position one bead on each side of the matchbox, leaving the other two beads approximately 1 in (2.5 cm) from each end.

3 Referring to the Basic Techniques section, attach the ends of your wire to a hook at one end and to your drill at the other and wind up the wires. You will then have a multicolored, three-strand wire cord.

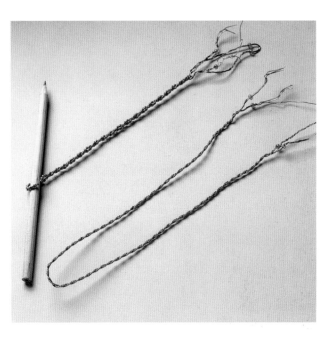

4 Remove the matchbox. Bend the corded wire in half, attach one end to the hook and the other to the drill again, and repeat the process so that you have a six-stranded cord.

5 Bend the wire in half again around a pencil. Holding the wire firmly at the other end, wind the pencil to form a 12-stranded cord. Repeat Steps 2–5 with each bunch of wires, so you will have five thick-corded lengths of wire.

6 Thread all five of the corded wires onto the pencil as shown above. With the pliers, grip the wires firmly about midway down and twist the pencil so that the cords at this end form into a thick rope—this will be the tree's trunk.

7 Spread out the ends of the cords to make the tree's branches. Bend and unwind some of them to give your tree character and to make it three-dimensional. Snip through the looped ends as shown above and trim off any excessive lengths.

8 To make twigs on the branches, separate out the ends of the colored wires where they emerge from the beads. Using jewelry pliers, curl each end around.

9 Take a large rounded stone and sand it clean. Thread some galvanized wire through the loop left by the pencil at the base of the trunk, wrap it around the stone, and twist the ends together with pliers. Repeat, using another wire at right angles to the first.

10 Cover the stone with foil, packing it around to form a pleasing shape. Make sure you flatten the base so that it will be stable.

11 Add half the 2-cut beads to approximately 3 dessert spoons of PVA glue—you may need a little more or less depending on the size of your base. Mix the beads in well—the PVA will become transparent when it dries, leaving just the beads on show.

12 Spread the bead mixture over one side of the base and leave to dry overnight. Then repeat Step 11 with the remaining beads and cover the other side of the base. Keep some mixture aside, covered with plastic wrap, to cover any areas where beads have come off or are a bit thin.

Luminous
lantern

The shiny inside of a cookie tin is great for magnifying the light of a candle. A hole has been cut in the top and a chimney added, to let out the heat, while the cap keeps the rain out. A pie dish creates a broad, stable base, while a small tin holds the candle. The protective mesh front cover is made from a heat spreader. These can be bought cheaply from a hardware store.

Other shaped tins can be used: square or hexagonal. Choose deep ones, because the back of shallow ones will get too hot.

YOU WILL NEED:

- Cookie tin
- Pie tin
- Small tin
- Small can for chimney
- 2 small bolts
- Galvanized wire 2 mm (8 gauge)

EQUIPMENT:

- Hammer and nail
- File
- Chisel
- Pliers
- Metal shears
- Riveter and rivets
- Heat spreader (flat metal mesh)
- Screwdriver and screw

1 Using a hammer and nail, make two holes in the side of the cookie tin close to the seam (this will be the bottom). One hole should be in the center of the side, the other 1 in (2.5 cm) nearer the top. Make two holes in the pie tin, one in the center and one 1 in (2.5 cm) away, and a central hole in the small tin.

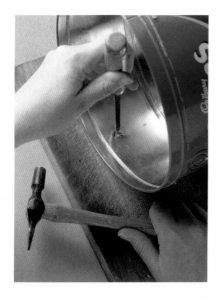

2 Place the tin that will become the chimney centrally on the outside of the cookie tin directly opposite the bottom holes, and draw a circle around its inside to mark its final position. Then position the cookie tin on a block of wood and pierce a "V"-shape through its side within the marked circle, using a hammer and chisel.

3 Use pliers to lift up this V-shape initially, which will give you space to get your metal shears in.

4 Cutting a neat circle is difficult, so do it slowly, working in a spiral with the tip of the shears. Then make a hole on either side of the circle with a hammer and nail, ½ in (15 mm) away from the edge.

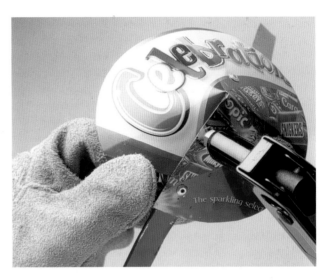

5 Draw a 6 in (15 cm) circle on a cookie tin lid and cut it out. Cut a 3 in (7.5 cm) straight line from the outside edge to the center of the circle, then wrap one cut edge over the other to form a cone. Mark two corresponding points on both the outside and the inside to fix the cone, and one point directly opposite. Using a hammer and nail, make holes at these five points. File the edges smooth and tape the cone from the inside to hold the shape, being careful not to cover the holes.

6 Cut a 12 x ½ in (30 x 1.5 cm) strip from the edge of a can lid. Bend this to fit inside the cone and mark through the two holes on either side of the cone to establish their corresponding positions on the strap. Make holes in the strap at the marked points and file them smooth. Then, using the riveter, attach the strap on either side.

7 Remove the lid and the base of the small chimney tin and hammer a hole midway on both sides. Bend the strap to fit inside, and mark through the holes to find the corresponding positions on the strap. Make two holes with a hammer and nail, file them smooth, and rivet the tin to a strap on each side.

8 Insert the straps of the chimney into the cut hole in the cookie tin. Splay out the straps inside the tin on either side and mark through the side holes already made to establish their position on the straps.

9 Remove the chimney and make holes in the marked points. File smooth.

10 Replace chimney and rivet it onto the large cookie tin attaching it to the strap on each side.

11 Position the pie tin on the base of the cookie tin, lining up the two holes and using an adhesive pad to hold it in place. Position the small tin inside, lining up the hole. Using longer rivets, attach the three tins together as shown, then put the second rivet through the other hole in the pie tin and cookie tin only.

12 Cut a length of wire to fit around the rim of your cookie tin, plus at least 6 in (15 cm) extra. Midway along this wire make an eyehole loop (see Step 15) using jewelry pliers. Looking from the front of your lantern, position this loop at the 9 o'clock position. Wrap the wire around the rim and twist the ends together to fix directly opposite the eyehole loop—both the remaining ends should be the same length. Curl these around with your pliers, as shown, to form two hinge loops.

13 Using a hacksaw, remove the handle from the heat spreader, and slide out and remove the remaining handle wire.

14 Cut a 7 in (17.5 cm) length of wire and form into a catch to go over the eyehole loop made in Step 12, using jewelry pliers. Slide the ends into the heat spreader to replace the handle.

15 Thread a length of wire through two holes in the mesh at the edge of the spreader, opposite the catch you have just made. Position the spreader over the cookie tin, fitting the catch in place, then bend the wires over the edge on the opposite side. Insert both through the hinge loops and bend around to fix in place.

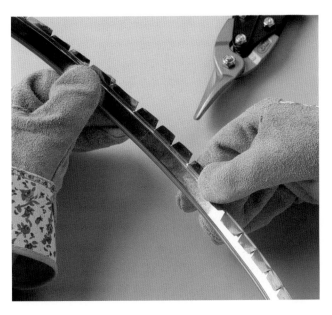

16 To make the handle, cut the rim from a tin or lid. Cut V-shapes in the cut edge as shown, wearing gloves to protect your hands. File any rough edges, then bend them over, hammering down if necessary. If the back of the handle is not smooth, line it with duct tape.

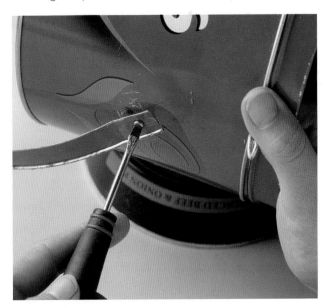

17 To find the exact balancing point for your lantern, once the mesh is fixed tie a string or strong elastic band around the lantern and suspend it. Experiment to find the exact points on the side to attach the handle to allow the lantern to hang true. Make a hole at this point in each side of the lantern and a hole at each end of the handle and file smooth. Line up the holes and attach the handle with small bolts.

Stunning
star

Metal stars similar to this one are used as traditional Christmas decorations in Scandinavia, but they look beautiful at any time of year. Hang your star in a corner of a room and the small pinpricks will make interesting patterns on the wall, while creating soft, warm lighting.

The pinpricks are made using a tailor's wheel. The template for this project is on page 122.

YOU WILL NEED:

- 2 sheets or a roll of 0.06 in (0.15 mm) copper foil
- Decorators' tape
- Padded envelope (or other yielding surface)

EQUIPMENT:

- Tailor's wheel
- Darning needle
- Ballpoint pen

1 Color photocopy the star template on page 122, cut out, and tape onto your sheet of copper. Place the copper onto a padded envelope. Using a ballpoint pen and ruler, emboss all the lines shown in red on the template.

2 Using the tailor's wheel, go over all the red lines, making sure the spikes are penetrating through the copper sheet. Don't go all the way to the points of the star with the wheel.

3 Remove the template and turn the sheet of copper over. Line up the template with your embossed copper and re-tape onto a fresh side. Then repeat Steps 1 and 2 on all the green lines. Using your ruler mark in all blue lines (don't touch the central red line). With a darning needle, pierce through each marked dot.

4 Cut out the star, making sure you go around the marked tabs. Then repeat Steps 1–4 with a second sheet of copper. This one doesn't need the tabs, so disregard them.

5 Gently but firmly form the star into its 3-D shape by easing the points of the stars towards each other sideways, thus forcing the midway lines to recede, as shown above. This is a difficult maneuver, so be patient.

6 Position your pair of stars on either side of your light/lamp and fix together by bending the tabs of one star around the star without tabs. Have the longest point hanging downwards.

Flowery
mirror

This bright and breezy mirror with its Mexican feel will enliven any wall.

It is easier to make than it looks. All the pieces have been cut out from an old cookie tin using the templates provided at the back of the book, colored in using permanent felt-tipped pens, and put together with simple paper studs.

The plastic frame was removed from an inexpensive mirror and attached to the back plate with double-sided tape. The flowers then hold it secure. You can hang it from a wire loop at the back.

YOU WILL NEED:

- Cookie tin (or chocolate tin lid)
- Cheap make-up mirror 4¾ in (12 cm) in diameter
- Permanent felt-tipped pens in green, pink, yellow, blue
- 4 in (10 cm) of wire
- Paper fasteners
- Mirror fixing pads
- Super glue

EQUIPMENT:

- Hammer and nail
- Tin snips
- Chisel
- Jewelry pliers
- Ballpoint pen

1 Cut open the round cookie tin using the tin snips, remove the base, and trim all jagged edges (see Basic Techniques, page 18).

2 Using the template on page 123, mark out nine flowers on the metal from the cookie tin sides and cut these out. Draw eighteen leaves to the size of your choice from the same tin, and cut out.

3 Place the template for the base (on page 123) onto the bottom of the tin and mark out the positions for the slots by firmly pressing into the metal with a ballpoint pen. With a nail, hammer a pattern around the edge of the base and on the leaves as shown.

4 Make sure that all the metal is very clean with no greasy finger marks, or the ink will not adhere properly. Then, using permanent felt-tipped pens, color the leaves in green, the flowers in pink with yellow centers, and the base blue.

5 Using the hammer and chisel, cut nine slots around your base at the positions already marked with the ballpoint pen. Then pair up each flower with a leaf and cut a slot in each pair with your chisel as shown, and then in each remaining single leaf just below the center.

6 With a hammer and nail make two holes, ½ in (15 mm) in from the edge and ¾ in (18 mm) apart. Cut a length of wire 4 in (10 cm) long, and bend it to form a loop. Thread each end through the back of the base to the front. Using jewelry pliers, curl around the ends of the wire to secure in, and form the hanging loop.

7 Using mirror mounting adhesive pads, attach the mirror to the base. Push a paper fastener through each flower and leaf pair and each leaf, as shown.

8 Fix the single leaves in position with the paper fasteners, in alternating slots around the base. Then attach the flower and leaf pairs to complete the surround. Add a dab of super glue to each of the paper fasteners at the back of the frame for extra security.

Recycled
tin toy

These charming and characterful cars are made from recycled ham cans. They can be used as fun ornaments or turned into "piggy banks" or paperweights by either cutting a slot in the top or filling with sand.

Other shapes and sizes of cans can be used. Look out for interesting ones—some cans look good without being painted—and colorful bottle tops to use for the wheels.

Trains can also be made by interlinking cans (pull ring fish cans make good traincars). These could be used to store paperclips, rubber bands, and other office materials.

YOU WILL NEED:

- I ham can
- Strip of card (size as wide as your can and enough to go all the way around)
- Double-sided tape
- Masking tape
- Enamel paint/spray
- Metal rod
- Piece of wide duct tape
- 4 bottle tops
- 4 small beads and 4 large beads
- Super glue
- Black permanent marker

EQUIPMENT:

- Hammer and nail
- Wooden block
- Scissors

1 Thoroughly wash the empty can so that no grease remains, and lightly sand the surface. Then paint, or spray, both the can and the strip of card. If you don't have duct tape for the windows, mask out the window shape before spraying. Leave to dry.

2 Mark two corresponding spots on either side of your car at the bottom of one edge for the wheel positions. Then, using a nail, hammer holes at each of these points on a wooden board or a protected surface. Make a hole in the center of each bottle top in the same way.

3 Cut out two pairs of shapes for the windows from duct tape and stick them in position. Outline them with black permanent marker. Alternatively, paint the windows in with silver paint and outline them with black pen, or paint a thin black line around the edge.

4 Using super glue, join the two halves of the car together and cover the join with masking tape. Then stick double-sided tape around the edges of the car, remove the backing, and position the strip of card around the edge, smoothing firmly into position.

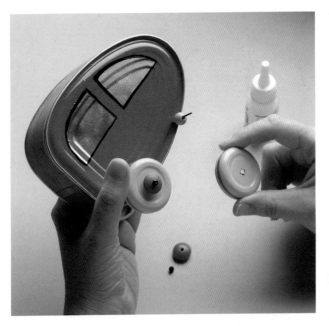

5 Cut four lengths of rod, each ½ in (15 mm) longer than the width of your tin. Glue a bead to one end of each to act as a stopper. Next, thread on a decorative bead, then a bottle top, then a suitable bead to hold the wheel straight and slightly away from the tin to allow the wheels to move freely.

6 Thread each rod through the holes cut in Step 2, adding beads and wheels in as in Step 5 but in reverse order to correspond to the other side of the car, gluing the final stopper bead in place. Snip off any excess rod once the glue has dried.

Butterfly
wall sconce

This candleholder, with its exuberant surround of colorful butterflies, is made from recycled beverage cans.

Beverage cans are easily cut into, exposing the silver inside. Use the templates at the back of the book to make the flowers and butterflies. Permanent markers have been used to color in all these elements.

The butterflies and flowers are attached by craft wire onto the aluminum wire frame. They could be used in bunches as gift ties or tags.

YOU WILL NEED:

- Aluminum wire 3.25 mm
  (28 gauge)
- Colored wire—super green
  0.315 mm (28 gauge) for
  antennae, 0.5 mm (24 gauge) for
  attaching butterflies
- 1 aluminum beer can (preferably
  silver in color) for holder
- 6 aluminum cans for the flowers
  and butterflies
- Permanent markers in bright
  colors
- Seed beads
- Removable putty

EQUIPMENT:

- Scissors
- Pinking shears (optional)
- Pliers
- Template photocopies
  (page 124)

1 Cut a 68 in (172 cm) length of wire and bend it at the midpoint around
your holder can. Bring the wire together and, using pliers, bend the wire
so that it meets and then heads straight away from the can as shown. This will be
the candleholder and its neck.

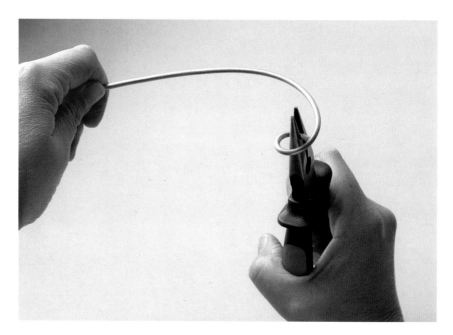

2 To make the sconce, refer to the Basic Techniques section, and form both
ends of the wire into an inward facing spiral.

3 Pull these spirals outwards so that when the inside edges rest against each other they form a heart shape, as shown. Bind this point together with fine wire.

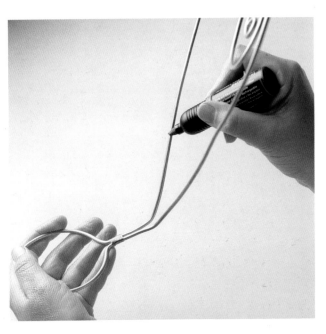

4 Bind together at the neck too. Then bend the holder at an angle to the heart, as shown. Color the wire forming the heart green, using a permanent marker, and the wire forming the holder in pink.

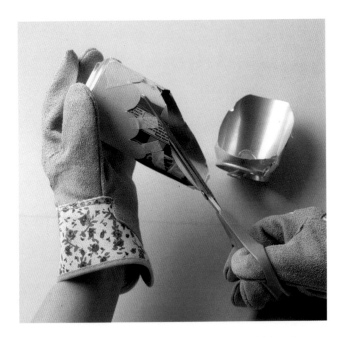

5 Copy and cut out the template on page 124 and tape it around the holder can. Cut it down to size as shown in Basic Techniques, page 19.

6 Cut around the outside of the heart with pinking shears. Then color in the heart, inside the can, and the scalloped edge. Using pliers, lightly bend down each scallop.

7 Cut open all the rest of your cans and pin them open on a wooden board. Copy the templates for the butterflies and circles (which are the flowers) on page 124 and cut out. Using removable putty, tack them to the metal and draw around them.

8 Cut out the butterfly and flower shapes. To complete the flowers, take the circles and cut small petals around the edge, as shown in the picture for Step 12. You will need approximately 22 flowers (9 large and 13 small), and 19 butterflies (2 large, 7 medium, 7 small, 3 tiny).

9 Color in the butterflies using permanent markers, making each one a different color and design. Use a large pin or a very small nail to pierce a pair of holes in the butterfly heads for the antennae, and holes at the neck and tail for attaching wire.

10 To make the antennae, thread a thin piece of wire through the head from front to back to front again and attach small beads to the two ends using jewelry pliers.

11 Using a thicker wire, thread the wire through the underside of the tail over the back and through the neck, looping through the antennae wire at the back of the head and closing the wire with pliers. Color all the flower petals in different shades and arrange them in three-tiered blossoms.

12 Pierce each flower through the middle. Cut 11 pieces of wire each 9½ in (23.5 cm) long. Attach a flower to each end by threading the end of the wire through the center hole of a flower, looping through a seed bead, and back through the center hole. Splay the end of the wire on the back to hold the flower on.

13 Wrap these pairs of flowers all around the heart sconce, alternating colors and sizes.

14 Attach the butterflies by winding the wire ends tightly in position on your sconce. If they keep moving, you can fix with a blob of superglue. Position the tin candleholder onto the wire frame.

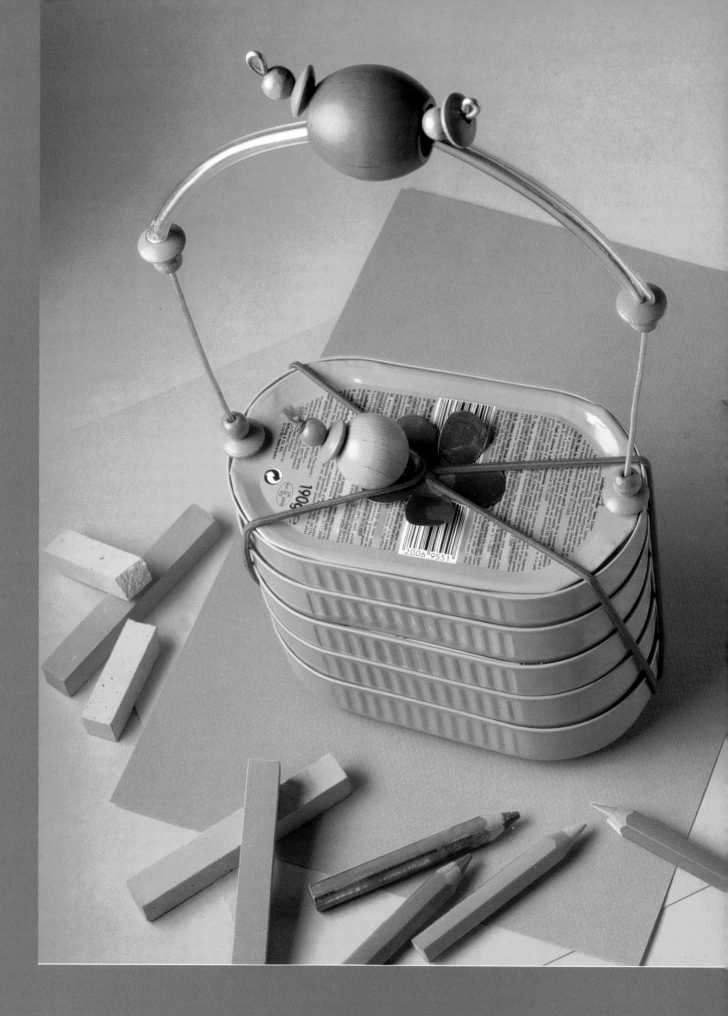

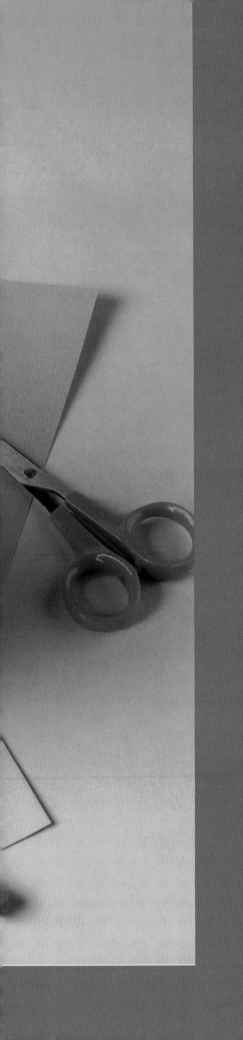

Bead holder

Recycled fish cans have been used to make this portable storage system. The cans have been pierced and threaded onto galvanized wires which have then formed a handle (with the addition of plastic tubing and beads).

    The holders are kept secure using pink elastic loops, which run from the base to the beaded flower knob. Unhook these, push the handle wires parallel, and the cans will slide up and down the wires. These cans could be used to store beads, crayons, seeds, or haberdashery items. Try different shaped cans for alternative storage systems.

YOU WILL NEED:

- 6 empty pull ring fish cans
- Round elastic in pink
- Wooden beads—7 green disk, 4 blue disk, 5 round pink, 2 turquoise blue, 1 large orange, 1 large yellow
- Colored eyelets
- Glue
- Galvanized wire 1.5 mm (14 gauge)
- Paper studs
- Plastic piping

EQUIPMENT:

- Darning needle
- Nail (slightly thicker than your wire size)
- Hammer
- File
- Craft knife
- Scissors
- Pliers
- Jewelry pliers

1 Mark points at the center of each narrow side of five cans, making sure they are all in the same position. Using a hammer and nail, make holes through each marked point from the inside out, as shown.

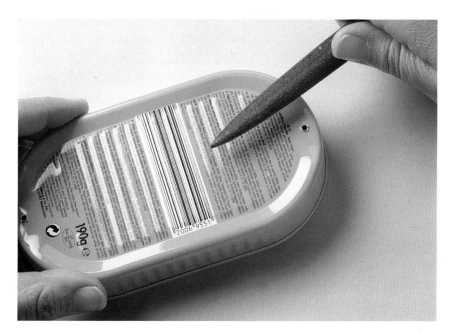

2 File the base of each hole smooth.

3 Mark the positions for the feet on one of the cans, then make four small slits with a craft knife wide enough for a paper fastener. Thread each fastener through a bead and then the slit and open them up on the inside of the can to secure.

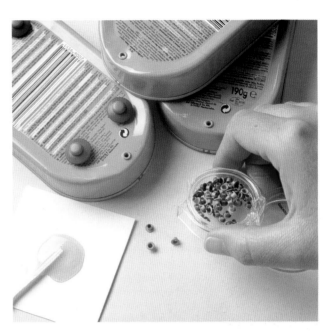

4 Glue eyelets into the holes in all the rest of the cans.

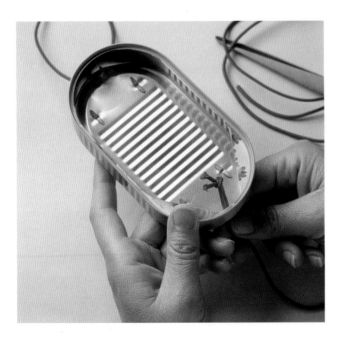

5 Make two loops of elastic, long enough to wrap around the piled-up cans, and knot the cut ends. Thread the loop through the hole in the base can (these holes may need to be made bigger than the rest) from the inside out, leaving the knots inside as shown.

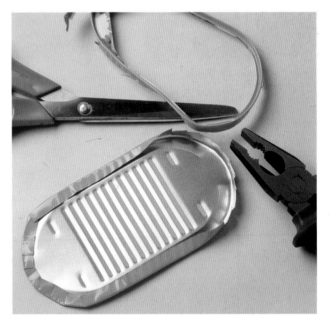

6 Remove the sides of the sixth can, cutting approximately ⅓ in (8 mm) away from the bottom edge. Cut vertical slits around the curved edges, then fold the edges in and clamp them down firmly with pliers. This will become the lid.

7 Make corresponding holes in the lid to line up with the rest of the cans. Using the template on page 123, cut out a flower from the pull ring lid, and color in with permanent markers. Place the flower on the center of the lid and hammer a nail through both pieces to make a hole. Knot a short piece of cord or elastic at one end and thread with five beads in the order: pink bead, green disk, large bead, green disk, pink bead, as shown. Thread the loose end through the hole in the flower and lid, pull tight, and tie a knot on the underside of the lid to secure.

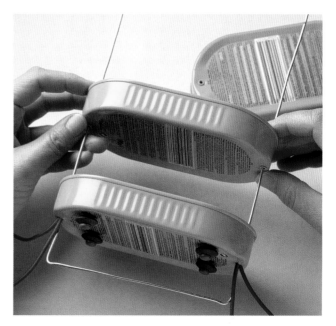

8 Cut a 36½ in (91.5 cm) length of wire and use pliers to bend approximately the last 15½ in (39 cm) on both sides at right angles, as shown. The midsection should be the same length as the space between the holes on the bottom of your cans.

9 Thread all five cans onto your wire frame, starting with the base can.

10 Thread on the lid and secure the cans by stretching the elastic side loops over the beaded knob as shown. Thread a green disk and a pink round bead onto the ends of each wire.

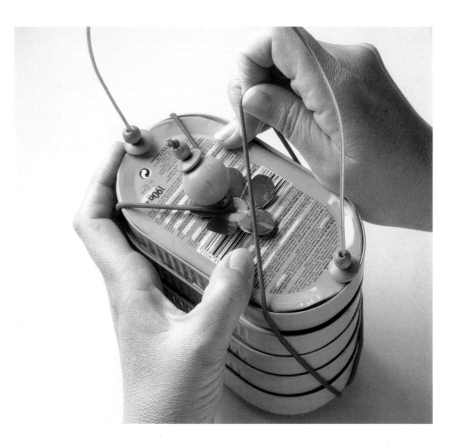

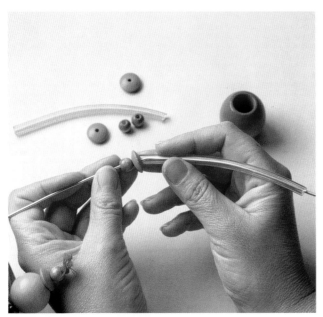

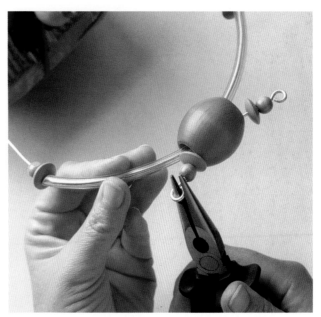

11 Thread a round pink and green disk bead onto each side and glue them into position on the wire 9¼ in (23 cm) up from the lid. Bend the wires at approximately 65° from the top of these beads and thread a piece of plastic piping 4½ in (11.5 cm) long onto each end.

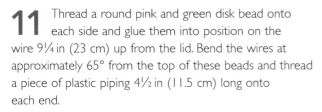

12 Then thread the ends of the wires through a large wooden bead from opposite directions, so that the wires cross inside the bead. Thread a green disk and pink round bead on to each wire and then curl the free ends with jewelry pliers.

Wire-mesh bag

This pretty bag could be used as a summer accessory for holding make-up and keys or, as suggested here, confetti for a wedding. It would also work well with evening wear.

The knitted wire is available in a variety of colors, so choose to coordinate with your outfit. The strap used here is made by stretching a length of the knitted wire, but ribbon or cord could be used as a cheaper option. The most difficult step is making the wire core at the bottom. It is worth practicing a few times before doing the real thing.

YOU WILL NEED:

- 7 in (17.5 cm) emerald green tubular knitted mesh 0.2 mm (30 gauge)
- 40 in (125 cm) super green (turquoise) 0.1 mm (32 gauge)
- 1 coil of super green craft wire

BEADS:

- 12 pink faceted
- 24 color-lined turquoise Rocailles
- 24 silver-lined clear Rocailles
- 36 turquoise bugles
- 12 small seed beads
- 12 frosted droplets
- 3 large-holed foiled beads (1 aqua, 2 violet)
- Nylon thread and needle

1 Cut a 14 in (35 cm) length of turquoise knitted wire and a 7 in (17.5 cm) length of green. Fold one edge of each over three times to make a 1 in (2.5 cm) cuff on the turquoise piece and ½ in (15 mm) deep cuff on the green.

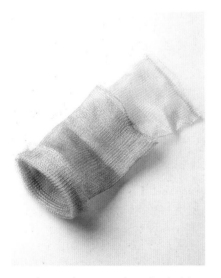

2 Insert the turquoise tube inside the green one and fold its cuff over the green cuff.

3 Place your index fingers inside the tube at both ends and grip with both your thumbs on the outside, then pull gently to shape the top of the bag.

4 Twist a tail in the end of the turquoise tube at the point where the green tube ends.

5 Gather together the end of the green knitting by making tiny pleats and pushing the wire together with your thumbs.

6 Make a small hook in the end of your 20 in (50 cm) length of wire and attach it to the base of the bag. Insert a pencil into your bag and use this as a former to wrap wire around. Try to make the coils neat and even.

7 Thread your large-holed bead onto the turquoise tail and glue in position just under the coiled wire. Then fan out the tail just below the bead.

8 With a needle and nylon thread, sew beads around the rim of the bag. You can do this by sewing each on individually, or by threading up a line and then stitching that to the bag. The first way is more secure, the second quicker. Stitch the bugle beads around the top (see the finished picture on page 94 for arrangement).

9 To make the strap, take a 39 in (100 cm) length of turquoise knitted wire and pull it, little by little, between your fingers until it has reached its maximum length. It will become a long slinky cord.

10 Thread a large-holed violet bead onto each end of the strap, then stitch the ends of the straps to the inside corners of the bag with nylon thread.

Wire-mesh
flowers

Made from fine tubular knitted mesh, these pretty flowers make a lovely posey which could be used as a bridal or bridesmaid bouquet, or simply placed in a vase. Alternatively, they can be made without long stems (just loop the wire around to hold the leaves in place, or stitch them together) and used to decorate a hat or wear in a buttonhole.

Knitted tubular mesh is available in two sizes: 0.1 mm (32 gauge), which has been used here to make the flower, and 0.2 mm (30 gauge), which has been used for the leaves. It is also available in a range of colors (see Wire-Mesh Lanterns, page 40), so you could have a variegated bouquet.

FOR EACH FLOWER YOU WILL NEED:

- 4 in (10 cm) length 0.1 mm (32 gauge) knitted wire in violet
- 2 in (5 cm) length 0.2 mm (30 gauge) knitted wire in emerald
- Galvanized garden wire
- Dark green Tanka wire
- One aqua bead with a 7/16 in (12 mm) hole
- One 1/3 in (8 mm) violet miracle bead
- One foiled 1/4 in (6 mm) blue miracle bead

EQUIPMENT:

- Wire cutters
- Darning needle
- Superglue
- Ruler

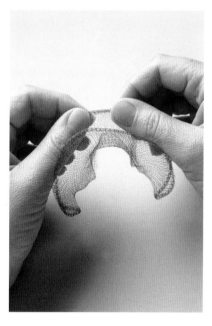

1 Cut a length of violet knitted wire 4 in (10 cm) long. Fold over the top four times, approximately 1/4 in (6 mm) each time. Press firmly around the rim each time you fold.

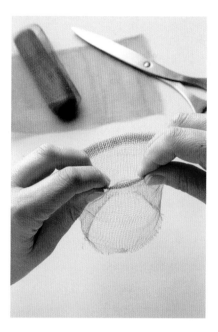

2 Stretch out the rim little by little until it reaches its maximum capacity. If it starts to unravel, you haven't turned it over enough times in Step 1.

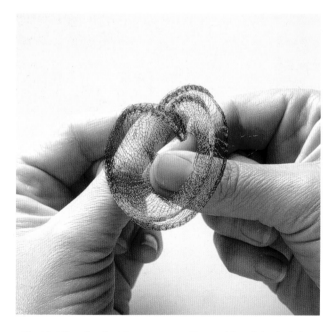

3 Holding the bottom corner of one side of the knitting, wrap the other side around to form a spiral, as shown above. Twist the base netting together tightly to hold the shape in place.

4 Force a darning needle through the center of the flower to make a hole. Glue the 1/3 in (8 mm) violet miracle bead to the end of a length of galvanized garden wire and thread the other end through the flower to form the stamen.

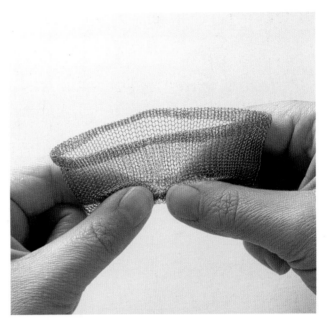

5 Thread the aqua bead onto the other end of the wire and push it up to the base of the flower. Using a twisting motion, carefully force it over the knitted core as shown. Thread the ¼ in (6 mm) blue miracle bead on after this and glue both in place.

6 Cut a 2 in (5 cm) length of emerald knitted wire. Fold over the top edge twice and press the fold firmly. Gather in the bottom slightly and fold over to join both sides together, pressing firmly. This fold will become the inner central vein of the leaf.

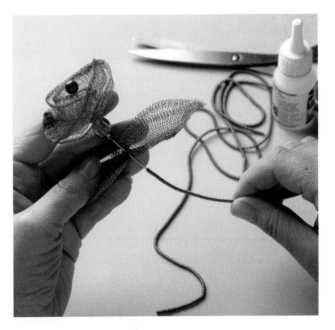

7 Pull and twist the middle section, as shown above, to divide it into two leaves. Once you have done this, shape the ends into pointed leaves.

8 Force a darning needle through the center of the leaves to make a hole and slide the leaves onto the wire. Cut a length of Tanka to fit the remaining stem and thread it on to cover up the bare wire. Glue the end to stop it from sliding off.

Wall
light

Copper and brass foil have been used to make this atmospheric wall light. The decorative pinpricks have been made with a tailor's marking wheel. The silver and brass disks are used both to join the brass edging and to make an eye-catching decoration. They are made from a combination of two types of paper fastener, which are available from office or art supply shops.

The light has been screwed to the wall, so it is a permanent fixture. When using household electricity, metal lampshades must always be grounded—if in any doubt, please consult a qualified electrician.

YOU WILL NEED:

- A 12 in (30 cm) square piece of 0.06 in (0.15 mm) thickness copper foil
- A 12 in (30 cm) square piece of 0.06 in (0.15 mm) thickness brass, aluminum, or pewter foil for the edging
- Eyelets (to fit paper punch size)
- Brass paper studs
- Strong double-sided tape
- Chrome paper studs with washers

EQUIPMENT:

- Paper holepunch
- Ruler
- Scissors
- Ballpint pen
- Bradawl (or pointed implement)
- Tracing wheel
- Hammer
- Eyelet ground wire (if using household electricity)
- Template pattern from page 125
- Decorator's tape

1 Photocopy the templates for the light on page 125. Attach the template for the main piece to the copper foil and the template for the edging to the brass, aluminum, or pewter foil with decorator's tape. Then cut out both shapes.

2 Remove the templates, and tape the brass edging to the copper as indicated on the template. Replace the main template and mark the positions for the holes firmly through both pieces of metal.

3 Tape the templates together and attach them to the metal with tape. Follow the lines on the template using a ruler and a tracing wheel. Do the scalloped line in freehand. Go slowly and carefully!

4 Remove the templates, separate the pieces of metal, and, using a paper holepunch, make holes at marked points in copper and brass edging.

5 Use strips of strong double-sided tape to attach the metal pieces together again, aligning the holes correctly. Fold back the side edges as shown on the template and go over them several times with a ruler and tracing wheel as shown.

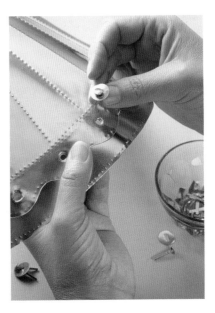

6 Insert a brass paper fastener through a chrome disk fastener, then fix into each of the row of holes across the top of your wall light. Leave the last holes at each end free, as these will be used to fix the light to the wall.

7 Spread each fastener's tail open to hold in place. Punch fixing holes at top and bottom or each side edge.

8 Attach an eyelet fitting— following the manufacturer's instructions—into the remaining holes at top and bottom on each side of the light.

9 If you are using household electricity you will need to ground the shade. You can do this by securely fixing a ground eyelet wire on with one of the eyelets at the base of the light. If in doubt, consult an electrician.

Tuna tin
shelf

Some cans are just so fantastic you don't want to throw them away. This classic tuna can, with its bold graphics and bright colors, has been recycled into a useful and charming little shelf.

Galvanized garden wire has been used to create the useful little hooks around the edge. Use them to hang your keys on, as here.

An alternative project, using the same type of can, can be found on page 111. There the can's rim has been attached to three lengths of chain to hang from a hook in the ceiling, and used for hanging kitchen utensils and bunches of herbs.

YOU WILL NEED:

- One circular can. The one used here measures 2 in (5 cm) deep by 6 in (15 cm) in diameter. Other sizes would work as long as they are not too deep.
- Length of 1.6 mm (12 gauge) galvanized wire

EQUIPMENT:

- Can opener
- Metal shears
- Pliers
- Jewelry pliers
- Hammer and nail

1 Remove the contents of your can via the base, leaving the top intact. Draw a center line across the top of the can and along this line hammer a row of little indentations with a nail, being very careful not to pierce the can.

2 Open the can around the edge from one end of this line to the other around the semicircle of the top you want to bend up. Brace a straight block of wood along the marked center line and push up the opened side as shown. This is a rather tricky maneuver, so be careful. The nail lines will help break the resistance and the wood will enforce a neater fold.

3 Measure around the rim of the unopened section, and mark equal divisions for six hooks. For each hook you will need four holes made in two pairs. Make the holes with a hammer and nail in each of the marked points, using a nail which is only slightly wider than the width of your wire.

4 Make two fixing holes at each end of the side piece, one at the top and one at the bottom. Then press these side pieces flat, so they form the lower part of the back of your shelf.

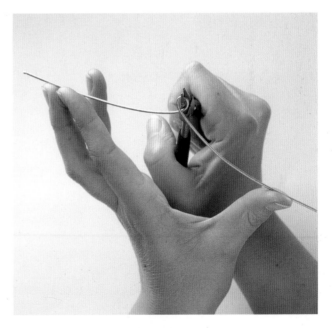

5 Using metal shears remove an approximately 3½ in (9 cm) wide section from the side of the can at the center of the back. You need to remove enough so that there is a small gap between the two ends when these sections of the side are pressed flat to form the back.

6 Cut six pieces of wire, each 9¼ in (23 cm) long. Mark the halfway point of each wire. Place the midpoint of each wire into the jaws of your jewelry pliers and wrap around, crossing the ends of the wires over as shown.

7 Bend the ends of the wires straight above the crossed point so that they run parallel to each other. Mark a point 1 in (2.5 cm) from the loop end.

8 Place a pencil against the wires at the marked point and bend them up around the pencil to form hooks. Repeat Steps 6–8 until you have six hooks.

9 Thread the ends of the wire on one of your hooks up through the two inner holes of one of the groups of four holes in the top of the can. Using jewelry pliers, loop each end of the wire outwards at a point ¾ in (18 mm) from the end, as shown.

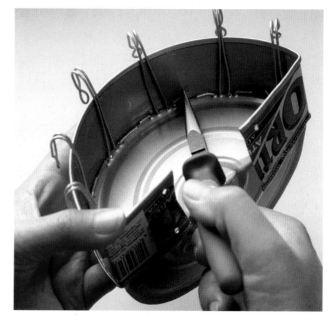

10 You may need to squeeze the loop together to make it narrower to fit the outer holes. Do this with ordinary pliers, then pull the wires back through the outer holes. Splay them out on the underside of the tin to secure. Repeat Steps 9–10 with the other hooks.

Hanging rack

1 For the hanging rack, remove the top and bottom of the can, leaving the side. Using 13 in (32.5 cm) lengths of wire, follow Steps 6–8 to make the hooks, but start by bending at 6¼ in (15.5 cm) from one end instead of in the middle. Place on the outside of the can and bend both ends over the top. The short wire will protrude a little below the rim. Bend the longer end around the front to the back of this and snip off any excess.

2 Repeat until you have nine evenly-spaced hooks around your can. Make three holes, evenly spaced, around the top edge. Through these thread on the ends of three galvanized metal chains to hang the rack.

Metallic
temple

This fabulous temple is ideal for special occasions, such as wedding anniversaries and christenings. It is constructed from an assortment of kitchen equipment, including empty food cans, baking pans, and graters, and held together with removable adhesive so that it stands securely but can be dismantled easily.

A specific list of materials is given here, but you can improvise with whatever you have at hand. We have used various battery-operated lights and torches to illuminate it. You could use fairy lights; consult an electrician if you want to use main voltage, as the metal temple should be grounded.

YOU WILL NEED:

- Square cookie tin
- 1 extra-large round food can
- Blu-tack
- 2 large round food cans
- 2 large, flat-backed, battery-operated lights
- Double-sided adhesive mounting pads
- 1 folding steamer
- 1 large and 2 small cheese graters
- 1 bicycle light
- 3 brioche baking pans
- 1 small nutmeg grater
- 1 key ring light
- Assortment of petit-four baking pans
- 2 wire pan scourers
- 2 collanders
- Tea-lights
- Small tin doll's house plates
- Shell-shaped madeleine baking pans

EQUIPMENT:

- Paint stripper
- Steel wool
- Pencil or fiber-tipped pen
- Square and round blocks of wood
- Vise
- Hammer
- Assortment of punches, nails, and chisels
- Metal file
- Protective gloves

1 If the cookie tin has a printed or painted finish, remove it with paint stripper and steel wool. Draw a pattern on the can with a pencil or fiber-tipped pen. Put a square block of wood into a vise to hammer against, place one side of the tin over the wood, and, using an assortment of punches, nails, and chisels, hammer out your design.

2 Draw arabesque windows and doors on the largest food can. Place a round piece of wood in the vise, and hold the can in position with removable adhesive mounting pads, and hammer and chisel out the shapes. Decorate the can by punching patterns around it.

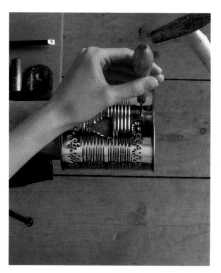

3 Repeat the same process on the two remaining food cans.

4 Smooth any sharp edges around the doorways and windows with a metal file. Wear gloves to protect yourself from sharp, jagged edges.

5 Insert a large flat-backed light into the base of the largest can and fix in place with double-sided adhesive mounting pads. Do the same with the cookie tin. Invert the cookie tin and place the inverted large can on top of it.

6 Invert the folding steamer on top of the round can, then put a large cheese grater on top of this. Put a small bicycle light in the grater. Top this with an inverted brioche baking pan and then a nutmeg grater with a key ring light inside. Finish the central tower with a petit-four baking pan.

7 For each side tower, place an inverted brioche baking pan on top of a punched round food can. Stretch a wire pan scourer around the base of a small cheese grater and place this on top of the tower. Add a turret of petit-four baking pans in diminishing sizes. To make the towers a little higher, stand each one on top of an inverted collander.

8 Once you have practiced putting the temple together, assemble it in the required location. Switch on each light and fix the sections together with removable adhesive mounting pads. To finish the scene, arrange tea-lights on small tin plates and back them with shell-shaped madeleine baking pans to reflect the light.

Tea
glasses

Simple, inexpensive drinking glasses
have been transformed into beautiful
tea glasses by the addition of an
elegant wire holder, making them
ideal for fruit teas, mulled wine,
or hot toddies. The flat shape of
the wire surround is achieved by
hammering galvanized wire. This is
a simple technique that produces
unusual and stylish results. For a more
elaborate effect, try using colored
glass and hammered copper wire.

YOU WILL NEED:

- 2.5 mm (6 gauge) galvanized wire
- Glasses

EQUIPMENT:

- Sheet of metal (to hammer onto)
- Hammer
- Wire cutters
- Needle-nose pliers

1 Place the sheet of metal on a sturdy surface and hammer along the length of the wire until it is sufficiently flat. It is best to do this in small sections because it is easier than handling long lengths of wire.

2 Cut the following lengths of wire for each glass: one to go around the top of the glass and one to go around the base (allow extra length for overlapping the ends); four lengths the same height as the glass to create two small ladders; two lengths to form a longer ladder for the handle (each one approximately twice the height of the glass); and six short lengths to create the rungs of the ladders. Add an extra ¾ in (18 mm) to the length of each ladder piece to allow for creating hooks to join them together.

3 First, assemble two small ladders, using the four glass-height lengths of wire and four of the short pieces of wire. Use needle-nose pliers to bend a small hook at each end of the longer wires, then use two short pieces of wire to join pairs of the longer wires together to form a small ladder. Use pliers to bend the ends of the short wires securely around the longer wires.

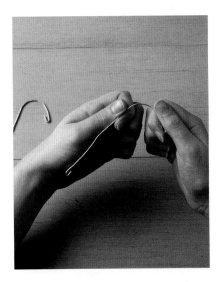

4 Make two circles of wire, one for the top of the glass and one for the bottom. Leave the excess wire in place because it will be cut later.

5 Use pliers to bend a small hook at each end of the handle wires, then use your fingers to form the wires into the desired shape. Make sure that both pieces are the same and join them together in the same way as the ladders in Step 3.

6 Using the glass to gauge the size, attach the top band of the glass holder to the handle by threading the ends of the band through the hooks of the handle. Use pliers to bend the ends back over the handle hooks to secure.

7 Attach the bottom of the handle in the same way, then cut off the excess wire from both the top and bottom bands. Use pliers to squeeze the ends firmly to create a secure fixing.

8 Attach the two ladders to the top and bottom band in the same way. Make sure the ladders are evenly spaced and that the ends are well squeezed together.

Templates

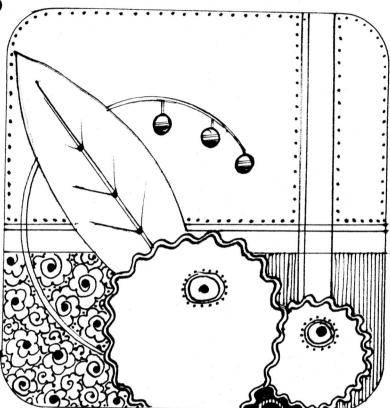

Pewter Coasters (pages 30–33)

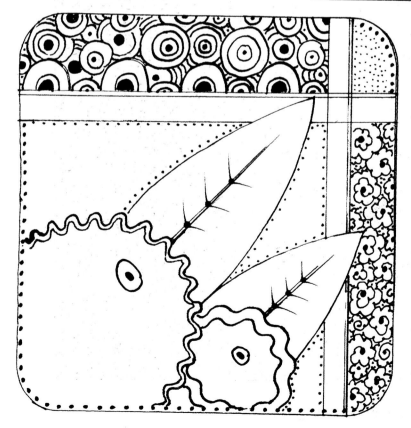

Embossed Tray (pages 54–57)

Stunning Star (pages 70–73)

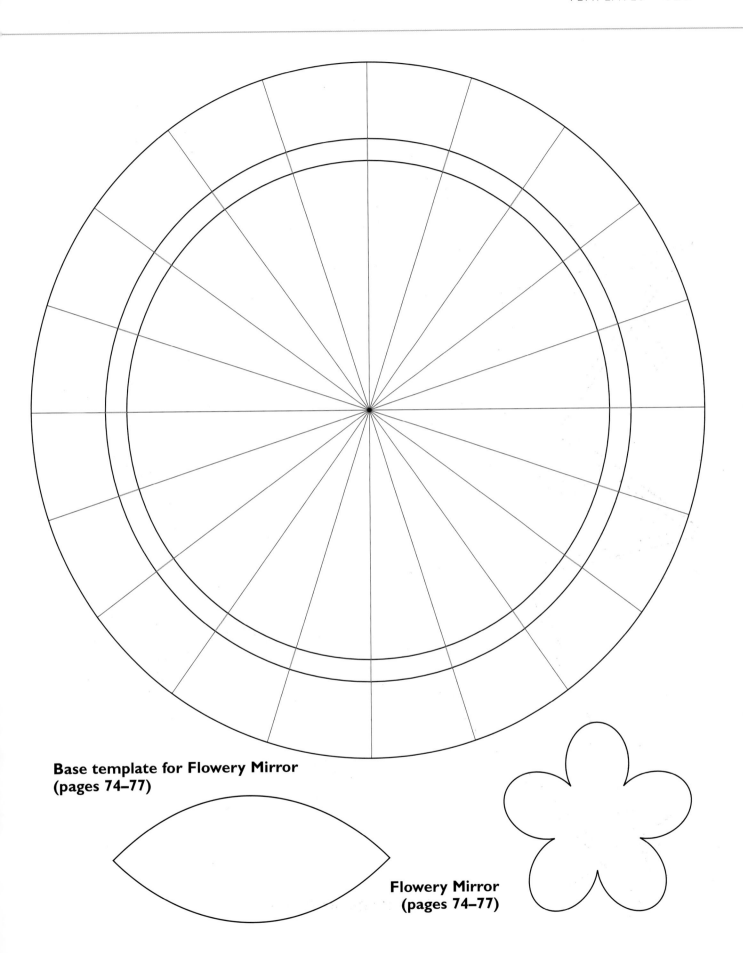

**Base template for Flowery Mirror
(pages 74–77)**

**Flowery Mirror
(pages 74–77)**

Foil Night Light Holders
(pages 24–29)

Note:
Templates on this page will need to be increased by 33%.

Butterfly Wall Sconce (pages 82–87)

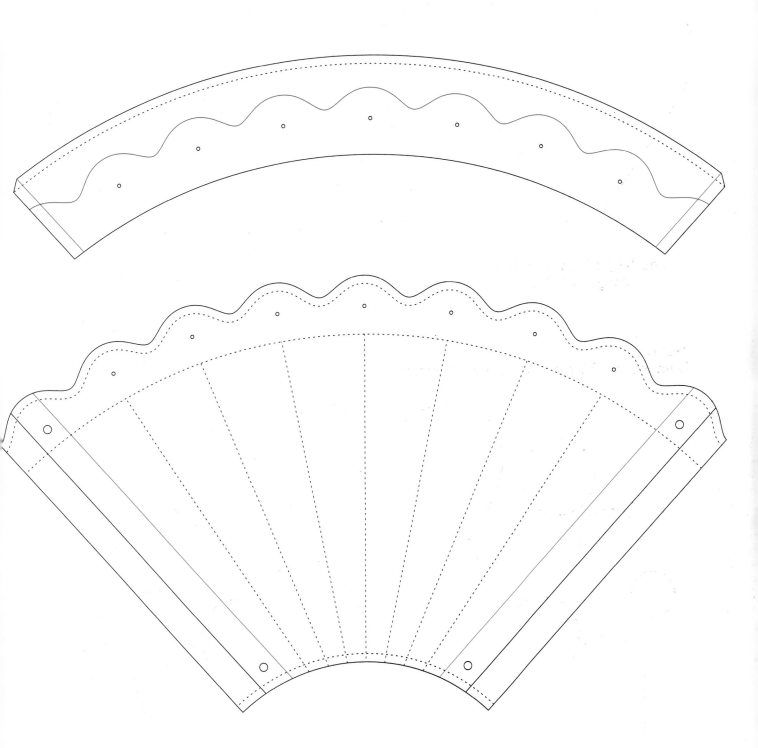

Wall Light (pages 102–105)

Index

Suppliers

CreateForLess
6932 SW Macadam Avenue
Suite A
Portland, OR 97219
1-866-333-4463
e-mail: info@createforless.com
web site: www.createforless.com

Creative Kits and Crafts
4326 Route 1, Suite 1
Monmouth Junction, NJ 08852
1-800-383-5487
e-mail: customerservice@kitsandcrafts.com
web site: www.kitsandcrafts.com

The Home Depot, Inc.
2455 Paces Ferry Road, NW
Altanta, GA 30339-4024
1-866-875-5488
web site: www.homedepot.com

Acknowledgments

The author would like to thank the following companies:
Fred Aldous—for supplying metal foils and embossing tools
The Scientific Wire Company—for supplying knitted craft and Tanka and spaghetti wire
Draper Tools Ltd—for supplying tools

The author would like to thank the following people:
Gracella—for being a lovely little model
Anne Wright—for extremely patient hand modeling
Libby Forbe—for supplying lots of interesting tins
Peter Williams—for his excellent photography
Georgina Rodes—for her thoughtful and inspiring styling